Saving Ginia

Also by Tracey-Anne Forbes and published by Ginninderra Press
Crushed Sugar

Tracey-Anne Forbes

Saving Ginia

Saving Ginia
ISBN 978 1 74027 873 7

tracey-anneforbes.webs.com/
Cover image: © WavebreakmediaMicro – Fotolia.com

First published 2014
Reprinted 2015

GINNINDERRA PRESS
PO Box 3461 Port Adelaide SA 5015
www.ginninderrapress.com.au

Contents

Part I

Lost

She seems so lost
My sister
So frail
Thin
As blue milk

When once she danced
Her feet
Nimble as a nymph's
Joy rode on her shoulders
And light spangled
From her hair
She raged
Music pumped
Mirror ball flashing
Furniture cleared
Carpet rolled
Drinks on ice
In the sink

It had to stop
I know it had to stop
Only sometimes
I wish
Her back

Only I know where she is
Only I miss her
Only I know why
She had to
Disappear

Childhood

We are twins
Ginia was the quiet child
Smaller, pale
With winter white hair
And solemn mouth
I was robust
Tumbling somersaults
While Ginia sat
Legs thrust out
Watching with her round blue eyes
Clutching Purry-Cat
Who poised
Limply tense
Ready to spring free

We grew like that
Me
The solid child
Good at games and science
Ginia muttering French
And fading with the afternoon
Behind ballet-class doors

She has never been loved by a boy
I know this
I watched, helpless
At her fumbled aching forays
Out
She was too private
Too frightened of the world
She retired into her tower

They call it Rejection Complex
Hey, I know
What she went through
I was there
I suffered too
Our parents loved us
But they were gypsies
Dragging us
Town to town
Country to country
School to school
Eternal outsiders

But I could cope
It was hard, yeah,
But someone had to take the knocks
To protect her
To save her
I could make friends
She couldn't
She was too sensitive
Crouching over her lunch
Slinking to the library
Watching with wide eyes
Hopscotch and skip rope

Now, I'm not so sure this was
A Good Idea
Perhaps I should have made her
Stand
Fight
Speak
Because she didn't
Speak
She wrote
Poems

Stones

Ginia loved stones
She gathered them
From Queensland playgrounds

As we moved from school to school
At first glazed hopscotch tors
Stones in their way

Watching with greedy eyes
The deft thumb-flicks of girls with
Fathers in the tiling trade

I had to barter from her stash
Of sea-tossed glass
Opalescent blues and greens

Filched from pebble beaches
On weekends at the sea
For tiles she had to have

Cerulean diamonds
Emerald squares
Ruby hearts

Then when we moved south
Along the coast
She found

Sea-polished marble
Moon-white globes
She placed in circles

Under her window
Some sort of talisman
Against the world

I guess
Although you never knew
With Ginia

Boyfriend

I cared for her
After our parents went away
She moved in with me and Jack
She hovered round our house
The garden
In the spare room when it rained
Jack
Didn't like her

Then she started to be wild
It sometimes shows in the poems
They mainly show her sadness
But she could be wild
Drink too much
Dance with the music
Cranked
Till the neighbours complained

And Jack couldn't take it any more

I'm the brisk one, see?
I'm smart and I work hard
Bring in the dough
Cook and clean
That's what the world wants, right?

Ginia couldn't cope with that.
That's why she locked herself away
To write her poems
That's why she came out at night
Raging to music
Dancing like a vortex

They're good
Her poems
I know they're good
She's my sister
And I have a certain bias
But they *are* good
They're all she has
They have to be

They made her happy

I helped her publish them
A small press
I spoke for her at the launch
We sold fifty copies
After, she was flat
We watched *The Hours* together
'You cannot find peace
By avoiding life'
I looked at her
But she gave me her secret smile
Twitched her head
No

Now, Ginia, I said,
Now, you have to
Live

She looked at me sadly
I frowned
She shook her head

I was thinking of her
Just thinking
When Simon came into the picture

Simon

Hey, the email said,
I've read your book
I have your address from your website
I want to say how much I like your poems
Can we meet?

A photograph attached
To show he's harmless?
Good-looking?
Because he is. In the pic
Which can lie

Hello, Simon, I replied
I'm sorry.
Ginia's no longer here.

But, came back,
Who are you?
Where has she gone?
She's not…

Look, I type,
I'm her twin. She's gone.
I check her mail. That's it.
I don't know when
She'll be back.
If at all.

I hesitate
I frown
I relent

But I'll meet you
To discuss her work
If you want.

First meeting

I meet him by the river
Jacarandas drip flowers like rain
On my face
Two ducks swim
One flips its head underwater
Slips water like mercury
Along its back
Flaps its wings so peacock colours
Flash
The day feels like summer
Air with a flick of heat
Cool sweat on the back of my neck
Under my fringe

I watch him approach
In long shorts and a polo shirt
His calves are fine and muscled
His eyes bay-blue
Long hands when he holds one out
Straight teeth
Flopping nutmeg hair

Jenny?

Yes.

Simon.

I know.

First scent

We find a café
I watch him
Guardedly
As he orders
For us both

He's thirty
Maybe

Confident
Eager
Smelling of tobacco-
Scent aftershave

A journalist
Smelling a coup
Maybe

A copy of Ginia's book
A notepad
A silver pen
On the table

Look, I say,
Why exactly
Are you here?

He shrugs
Smiles so a dimple forms
In his chin
So light glints
In his baby blues
I find your sister
Fascinating
I want to make a film
About her

O
K

Find out
What's behind the poems
There's a market for this
She'd get a cut
Of course
If I can sell the doco

And it'll sell her new book
'Cause she's working on a new one
Right?

Innocent eyes
Innocent dimple

Twins

Are you identical?

I shake my head
Laugh
Only in looks
But I know her poems
Intimately
Know where they were written
When
Who about
What sort of doco
Do you have in mind?

He leans forward
Intent
His eyes with the shine of seawater

Well, for starters
I want to film the places in the poems
Then voice-over the text
Get her to voice-over the text

I'm staring at him
As his coffee cools
He's finding a poem
In the book
Open on the table
He's absorbed
As the world grinds on
An electric saw screaming
In a house being built
Hiss, grind and smash of garbage truck
Swish of traffic

Then
A bit of analysis
Where the poem came from
What was happening in her life
At the time

I think she might become

An

Important

Poet

You can't be serious

I'm staring at him
I'm frozen
I can feel the blood
Burning
In my shoulders

Fuuuuck!

You can't be serious!

He looks at me
Head on one side
What?
Of course I'm serious
She's good
Sometimes she's
Freaking
Fantastic

He's busy
Sorting through
The poems

We could start with
'Tallebudgera Creek'

Tallebudgera Creek

Canopy of jungle limbs
like Brontosaurus necks
twisted in tortured knots

Rocks splotched with fungus
like splashed bird droppings
a tumble of grey boulders
brooding
dangerous as dozing rhinos

Surfers Paradise is a town
veiled in mist
crystallised
turned to jagged bars of salt
like the wife of Lot

There is a briny stink to the sea
water from a drain
inks the grey slosh with brown stain

Blue fishing nets strain soft drink bottles
crushed beer cans
and matted leaves
The waves lift like glass
flop like filth

At the estuary there's a groyne of sandbags
layered like bricks
to frame the fretful sea

They have skins like hairy coconuts
fuzzy and warm
bread-loaf brown
with a dusting of pepper

Across the frothing foam
the peninsula is wild –
scrubby mangrove trees
and a biscuit stretch of beach

To the lighthouse
like a still, tall man
staring out

But the sky
is empty

Analysis

What did she mean,
The sky is empty?
What was she looking for?
People want to know
They want to know the poet
Behind the poem
What the poet was aiming for

I press my lips together
Shake my head
But that's the point of poetry
The guessing game
The mystery behind the lines
The readers finding meaning
For themselves

He smiles
Indulgently
Yeah, right
In the twenty-first century?
In the time of
Reality
TV?

He leans forward
Eyes bright
Look, I have money
From another film I made
I had an Arts grant
Sold my doco to the ABC
I know they'd buy this one too
This could be big
Really big
Make lots of money
For her
Sell her books

Make lots of money
For *you*

A smirk
That too

Relationships

And then we move on
To relationships

That's the meat
For the punters
That's the gory detail
They want

He finds
'Frailty'

Frailty

Silver light
flicking through my fingers;
the teapot breathes a white wisp of steam

the morning
stretches like a lazy body
browned from holidays and warm nurturing…

The afternoon
is less certain.

Having eaten of my soft heart,
will you leave me
on the balcony in the sun
empty
as morning eggshells?

An ex

This one, for instance,
Is so sad
So full of insecurity
Who was the boyfriend?
What went wrong?

The blue inquisitive flash
Of his eyes

I stare at him
Breathless at the irony
He's missed

I look down,
Stir my own coffee
Reflect on what
Or what not
To say
Catch those baby blues
Again

She fell in love,
I say slowly,
Over and over
Had her heart broken by men
Who had no idea
They had blood on their hands
They used her…
I stare at him intently
But he still doesn't see it

He shrugs
So it's a way
Of getting back
At them

I watch him
He's turning pages eagerly
Finding another one
I feel my own heart
Somersault
I watch his hands,
Slender, searching
I press my lips together

I will not let this happen
I will not let this happen
I will not let this happen
Again

Night vision

The blue-black hard grittiness, edginess
– my soul grating on yours:
your pain withdrawing, eyes burying their hurt,
their lashes curled like fingernails
at the shriek of metal upon metal –

In the three o'clock darkness
I listen to the house start
and the trees moan;
breath puffs around me like powder
drifting from a fading ghost;

but you are real and turned away
and only the moon-white hairs
on your satin-skin back
stir dreamily
at my breath

and the sad soft sighings
of our frail faith.

Another ex

That sounds like someone serious
Do you know who that was about?

I shrug
Sure. But he's long gone
Like her

I sit up straight
Become brisk
Look – you're wasting your time
I can't keep answering for her
You'd have to speak to her

Jenny – that's what I want!
But you said she's disappeared…

Yes.
Yes, I did

But surely you –
Her twin –
Must know where she is?

I shake my head
Fumble in my purse for coins
Even as he's saying
No, don't be silly…

Look – you're wasting your time
She went on antidepressants
Now she's disappeared

But – how? When?
His eyes blaze at me
Oh, goddam…

I pull myself together.
It's not that easy
She was sick
She's gone away to get well

You say she was depressed?

Acutely
Couldn't you tell
From her poems?

So was Woolf

I raise an eyebrow
Grimace
And look what happened
There
Forget her

But you can't just let her
Disappear!
This could make her famous
Really famous!
Give her the way
To keep writing!

You've come along too late
No one else cares…

What about you?

Got me there.

Sunday

A white-filmed sky
Still, cool air
Long shadows
A jet cruising slowly past
Loan shark

A cushioned cane chair
Bright new leaves on the potted lime
White veranda rails
Terracotta tiles
Flashing palm trees

Ginia.

I sigh
I open her book
Sift through pages she wrote
Before she started to fade
Before the pills took her
Before she was gone

Sea-made

There is nothing, you say,
in the liquid sleep of curling dreams

We can't connect –
my mind sailing on the swell of scented wind
yours dry and stiff and anchored to the concrete

I am ephemeral –
you can't catch me –
but you try –
I resent that above everything.

I will not be what is expected of me:
something has snapped
and I am adrift

on a lilt of latitude
floating far from your furled umbrella minds
safe and sunny from your 'sanity'

so free,
so strong,
so dangerous

Wild

I nod
I remember her
Like that

It was after our sister died

She was wild
Out of control
She lost her licence
Was losing her job
Was losing her mind

She cut her hair
Dyed it blonde

Peroxide blonde

When I turned twenty-five
I went blonde –

no longer afraid of consequences
and wild-at-heart in an unwild world –

no one liked the straw-bright highlights
the strands of chestnut changed to copper-gold,
nor my new indulgence in black vinyl…

re-invention is an outrage
in the lanes of narrow minds

But I go my defiant way
riding on a cloud of fine-

ite
            caution to the wind

Down

Then she was down

Nothing could rouse her
I cooked for her
I cleaned
She lay about
Listless
Staring at Jack
Staring at me
Turning her face
Away

Writing
Bleakly

Winter morning

The light is shatter-bright
dew scattered shards
from the sun's swift fist

But suburbia murmurs
in muted coos
and mumbled moans –
pigeons and drivers
musing both
on dreary lives
and freezing fingers

and the teapot sighs
its breath a lazy genii
roused to wake

a heart
not in it.

Winter-dark

The winter afternoon
settles like mist
bumpy white sky
stiff stems of fronds and fern
waving vaguely –
uncertain relatives

expecting rejection

Cold wind outside
thick glass
white sheets flickering
like frightened eyelids
gum leaves fluttering
nervous hands

fearful hearts

Blue, blue light at dusk
wet courtyard silvered
roof steely
from blue-grey sky
wet table black-brown
plastic chairs white-blue

And just those two
next door
roar of football
greasy smell
of lamb
sour taste
of loneliness

Sunflower

Petals brilliant yellow –
the yellow of butter –
open unsteadily
as a new-born calf
trying to stand

The green centre
as intricately whorled
as a spirograph
the baby seeds
purple points

The stem
is thick and fuzzy
but the leaves
less certain
two ragged with holes

a beetle, small as a bee
with green iridescent wings
a yellow spider
a black ant
scuttle
The petals
might be a child's bonnet
frilled around a face
tightly laced
frowning at the sun

A week later
the head is heavy
I lift it in my palm
It lolls, pregnant
with seeds and sadness

When I release
my fingers gently
it stares sombrely at the grass
Waiting perhaps for birth

Or death

Lancelot

That was two years ago
She was coming slowly back
Was on the mend
When she fell in love with Lance

It's not his real name
It's what I call him
Because his was the final sword
To tear her healing heart
Apart
Again

To rip the frail fabric
Of her stirring faith
Her stirring hope
Her finally stirring dreams

On my wall I have a painting
Dark Lady of Shallot
A black-skinned lady
Hibiscus in her hair
Floats in a bark-boat
Behind

A white-sailed yacht
Where fair Lancelot
Holds sway and
Smiles dreaming at his harbour
Of scattered cabins
And busy white-skinned men

The dark lady twists
One hand out-stretched
Her yearning face
Reflected in the sea
In the still, green, concave mirror of
A shiny slip of after-wave

But a ridge of foam
From the yacht's wake
Is curled to smash her glass
To smithereens

And so Lance did
To Ginia

Cold

It was bad then
Jack became cold
He didn't know
Why she had tipped again

He didn't have a clue
About Lance

All he saw were her wild eyes
Her mad tears
Her empty spells of wordless
Pain

It is too much
He said
I can't do this
Again

I don't want her here
I can't have her here
It's you I want
Not her

Choice

So I had to choose
Between them

Our parents had retired
Into grief
Left us, to live on Stradbroke Island –
It was where they met each other
Mum in white shorts
All long brown legs and pin-tossed hair
Dad in a broad-brimmed hat
White cotton shirt
Solemn, head full of physics
Till he saw her

You couldn't blame them –
They loved us of course
But they had each other
And I had Jack
And Ginia had me
And Tess had
Had
No one

Except our
Lost parents
Who couldn't
Comprehend
Who couldn't
Get over
Who couldn't
Not
Wake in the morning
To the same
Nightmare

Tess's skirts
Hanging empty
Beside empty blouses
Empty jeans
Empty coats

Her empty bed
Her empty shoes
Her empty room
In their emptied lives

Ginia had no one else
You see?

I had to choose

Ginia

My ex

It was bleak
Jack and I
Gave up our house
I needed to shift my stuff

It was raining
I didn't want to meet him
But he was there
At the house
With a truck

I'd boxed up my books
Packed my suitcases
Taking a bed, a dresser
A table and some chairs
Kitchen stuff
My stereo

Light fell through rain and dusty glass
In Mum and Dad's old place
He helped me dump my stuff
In the hall
He looked at me
Grimaced
Well, I guess this is it

Yes.
He became blurred
Green light through trees and rain
Swam through rippled glass

I watched his car drive away

I washed down walls
Cleaned the windows
Mopped the timber and tile floors
The radio sang

Time it was
Time it was
It was a time
Of innocence

I flopped on the mattress
Wept

Pulled myself together
Unpacked the kitchen
Hung clothes in cupboards
Picked up pizza
And red wine

Fetched Ginia

Time to change

When the wine was gone
I took a breath
Now, I said,
This time
You need to listen to me
You need to stop this
You're killing yourself

Poetry isn't worth it
You see what it's done to you?
To me?

She stared at me
Her blank eyes
Teal with fear
We're going to the doctor
Tomorrow

She cried
She screamed at me
She smashed a glass
She scared me
She scared herself

She listened to me

Her blood pressure was bad
Her blood tests were bad
The doctor prescribed
Antidepressants

It will take two weeks
Before they starts to work
Before you start to feel better
Give it time, he said

He gave her a month off work
Diazepam
To get her through
To get me through

Over those weeks
Her poetry began to change
And she began to fade

Neutral

A handful of crows
fling like black soot
from the chimney next door

I lie swathed in green steam
my white body prone,
hands floating
useless

in the milked tiles
a ghost-face
turns

web-threaded blinds
angle at impassive clouds
and a sheet of weatherboard

windowless

...

A swallowed pill
creeps the panic
from the morning –

the drawer's mouth
breathes sawdust and glue
new

as my mind becomes
with the grainy grey
dissolving

pain
shadow-slinking
bad cat

numbed
etherised
shut with the drawer

out of sight
out of mind
out, out…

Can I really bring her back?

I put away her poems
Iron clothes for work
Cook a meal
Wash dishes

Check our email

He's insistent
He won't take no
He's emailed me
Relentlessly

I know her poetry by heart
I have to meet her
Please

I don't answer

I go to work
Write reports
Answer phones
Type mechanically

Buy his last film and watch it
Am favourably impressed

Check our email

Give her a chance
To speak for herself?
Come on Jenny
You owe it to her
To the world

Drink coffee
Stare blankly at my screen

I don't know him
He could be a stalker
He is a stalker
Stalking Ginia

But deep down I know
She'd love it

Maybe it *is* time
For Ginia
To come back

Asleep

I find her in the dark

Creep into bed with her
As she sleeps
I stroke her arm
And she twitches
Limply

Should I wake her?
She seems so peaceful
The lace bodice
Of her nightdress
Softly rising
Softly falling

She *is* peaceful
The first true peace
She has ever had
But she is only half-alive
Or half-dead

Telling her

In the morning I wake her
Tell her about Simon
Tell her about the doco
Ask what she thinks

I see a weak glimmer
In her faded eyes
Feel her limbs stir
Stretch
Shiver

See her hands go to her mouth
Her eyes widen like a cat's

And then I drop the bombshell

Simon wants more poems
New stuff
A new book to promote
With the film

You need to write again

She closes her eyes
Opens them to her pale nightdress
To her thin limbs
To the pile of empty paper beside the bed

She takes my hand
Squeezes it
Hard

Agree

I email Simon
I've talked to her
She can't see you yet
But I think she likes
The idea

He shoots back
Yes! Oh yes!
I knew she'd agree!
Thank you Jenny!
Thank you!

She thinks you should start
The beach filming
Then she'll decide
And she wants
No one named

Anything!

I'll tell her.
I stare at the emails
In my inbox
At the papers
In my in-tray
At the clock ticking over

When are you thinking
Of starting?

Oh – do a trial start
Soon as I can
Maybe two weeks
While the light's
So good
While the weather
Holds.

Mind if I come
With you?
The first day?

Silence.
Then: sure, why not?
But I warn you
It's a long, long day.

No problem.

Picking him up

It's a Tuesday
I take a sickie
I work in government
They won't miss me
My emails will still be there
On Wednesday
My work in its in-tray
That never empties

I tell him I'll pick him up
He objects
Says he'll drive
Folds at my crispness

I want to see his place
See where he lives
Find out what I can
Before Ginia
(If Ginia)
Meets him

He lives in a block of units
At Hill End
Near the river
Flashy

Why would I have expected less?
He's told me he freelances for a newspaper
In between jobs
Makes his own hours

Talented?
Good enough to capture
The real
Ginia?

Driving to the coast

She knew about phoniness

He's reading
'Peroxide Blonde'

I take a breath
Concentrate on the road
Shrug
So?

Is she still blonde?

I flick a glance at him
Move the car into the right lane
No
She's back to being chestnut
I think it was a regression thing
She was blonde as a baby
I told you
She had mental
Issues

She's a teacher, right?

He's reading
'Part-time in Arabia'

Part-time in Arabia

I am a nomad teacher,
hauling my arm-load of knowledge
to the brinks of their twitched tent-minds,
placing my thoughts in neat piles before them,
in lines of ink for them to sniff suspiciously,
in words
which cascade like strange music –

And sometimes I am allowed to enter
the frail walls of their minds,
to leave my gifts
and take the humble payment
of whatever their eyes
have the language to express.

Teaching

Was
They sent her off out bush
Where she wrote that
It was after a better day

Some days she could cope
But most she couldn't
It was killing her
They were eating her alive

She wouldn't have survived the year
Even if…

I lugged her back
I stopped her teaching
I told her I would
Look after her

But –
What about your parents?

Parents

They're gone
They retired to Straddie

I don't look at him
I stare at the road
Slow automatically

After our sister died in a car crash
It was while Ginia was out west
Tess was driving there to see her…

Out, out, I think:
Out, out, brief candle…

Out, damned spot…

Starting to get nervous

I'm telling him too much
Personal stuff
And I know next to nothing
About him

Oh my God, I am so sorry…

My hands twist
I squirm
Refuse to catch his eye
Shrug
It was a while ago
We were twenty-four

I listen to his silence
Catch his face
In my glance
Frown

What else
Have you got there?

After a moment
A rustle
The quiet shuffle
Of pages

Then cautiously:
This 'Cerise' one
Mind if I read it
Out loud?

Cerise

So many things I can recall –
glossy wallpaper with furry felt roses
an attic roof
diamond-paned glass

The cherry tree,
covered in fluff-blossom
tiny buds blooming
bunches of ruby fruit

Picked cherries
preserved in eau-de-vie, distilling
liqueur, pale pink
fragrant with summer

cherry jam,
thick and chewy, gushing syrup
staining our mouths
blood-red

The whisper of clothes in the dark
the creak of her bed

Getting too close

Do you know who the 'her' is?

I nod. Take a breath
Take a risk
It was a woman from a poetry class
She invited her for a holiday
Down south one spring
It was nothing

It doesn't sound like nothing

I wince
She took love where she could find it
But not even a woman
Ever loved Ginia
The way she wanted

Except me, I think
It was why I had to help her
Disappear

I can't tell him that
I can't tell him about that

Yet

I catch his gaze
Curious
Intent

I can't tell him about that
Perhaps
Ever

The beach

We stop at Burleigh
Salt breeze whips hair
Across my face
Whips white peaks on the waves
Like in her poem

Simon rubs his hands with glee
Unpacks his gear
How would you like
To read the poem
While I take some film?
See how it works?

Burleigh Beach

By day the waves
stream flying manes
hooves crash under them
like symphonies

Seagulls stand in the hurling wind
feathers ruffled like fur
beaks snapping like castanets
when they speak
they creak

… But at night the sea
slides in like a violin,
swings out like a dance skirt
with a white lace petticoat

In sandals sand slips
chill and sudden as a cello
and the wind
whispers
like a wing

First film

He films waves
Seagulls
Sand
The headland

The light is crisp
Spring-fresh
The sky as blue as his eyes
No clouds in either

We'll need classical music
In the background
We'll need to come back
For the night shots

Now it's 'we'

But he hasn't noticed
He's absorbed
Thinking
Replaying film

Listening to my voiceover
Caught in the wind
In the crash of waves
In the scream of gulls

What's next?

'Tallebudgera Creek'

Any chance of a swim
First?

Checking him out

I have my bathers
Under my jeans and shirt
He's wearing boardies

I don't slip on a sun-shirt
Even though it's late morning
Even though it's late spring

He hesitates
Shrugs
Pulls off his polo

I like the straightness of his shoulders
The dimples above his butt
His careless winter-paleness

He sees me looking
And is looking too
I turn to the sea to hide my blush

Gasp as I dive
At sheer cold shock
At sheer cold possibility

Break

We grab a bite
In a café
He's excited by his footage
I can see that
In his restless movements
His brisk sandwich order
His shot of short black

These beach ones are great
He says
A great way to get the viewers
In
Let's try for three today
'Tallebudgera' will be tricky
With the gear
'Fingal' should be easier

I nod
Sip a flat white
Try to stay focussed
Try not to catch his eye
Too often
Look at him
Too much
Let's do 'Fingal' first, then

He considers
Looks it up

At Fingal

The great ocean sweeps in long beach breaks to the sand
Spray in fistfuls flings at the bluff

Gulls swoop and squabble, dive, scream, hover, squawk and
flock like flies to trapped fish in teal troughs
swing skyward in tandem like paper planes
caught and linked by wind and misted salt

The sand on the boardwalk to the lighthouse is grey
redolent with childhood pepper-scent:
minerals and casuarinas, salty skin.
Spiky pandanus with flute-nuts

stand stiffly to the sun
guarding the quiet paths to caves of cool

Not so easy

'Fingal' is not a success
Though:
There are no fish
No swooping gulls

He makes notes
Checks tides and weather
On his phone
Fiddles endlessly with his gear

I begin to understand
The work that will go into this
Begin to understand
He needs Ginia

Before he can commit
His time
His energy
His full focus

I begin to realise
This is not just flirtation
This is not just a day at the beach
This is not just a hobby thing

We don't even make it to 'Tallebudgera'
Before the light begins to fade

I'll be in touch

I drop him off in the dark
Sand and salt and heat in my hair
On my skin

I help him unpack the gear
In the car boot's light I see him hesitate
I'm suddenly skittish as a kitten

I'll be in touch
Once I've talked to Ginia
Again
I promise you
I'll do my best
To talk her into it

I'm looking up at him
My voice rushed
Breathless

He nods, smiles
Thanks Jenny
And for everything today

I smile back
Shrug
My pleasure

See you then

See in my rear-view mirror
He's watching me

Go

Serious

Back home I heat leftovers
Take a glass of wine to my veranda
Palm fronds move in the dark air
Glint in street light
A possum rustles gum nuts
Jasmine scent winds like smoke
From the heavy hedge

I don't know what to do

Simon's serious
He's absolutely serious
About the doco
I know that
Now

But Ginia's calm
She's better than she's ever been
She's not torn apart
By restless longing

Even though she can't write
At least she's not writing
Like she was writing
When we lived with Jack

In our big house
With our big garden
In the big quiet silence
Of her pain

Tears

Ginia doesn't cry any more

She used to cry every day
Every day
Sometimes three, four times

Now she never cries

We went to a funeral
In a Polish church
A full requiem mass

The priest sang so mournfully
Everyone cried
Except Ginia

She looked up at the high white walls
The lit chandeliers
The whirling fans

She hummed to herself
Closed her eyes in the Polish hymns
Almost fell asleep

She used to cry at sunsets
She used to cry in movies
She used to cry at violins

Ginia doesn't cry any more

But…

But what if she is better?
After all, she has been well
Been cheerful even
Working for a gardening firm
Rising early, sleeping early
Watching bouncy game shows
Instead of morbid news

The tablets have transformed her
Made her calm and steady
Made her mind white-bright
Instead of murky-dark
With sudden prism flashes

But I've caught her unawares
Once or twice
Holding a pen over a page
Her eyes blank
With sadness

Can we risk it?
I go to my room
Take her book from a shelf
Open it
Remember again what she was like

Numb

The TV has a honey patch
of sun
dappled with gum leaves

The wind is hot and pungent

I point my ballerina toes
in the elbow light
stand poised as I did in the Elementary exam
my ankles still thin
my calves carved
knees knotted

White anklets the sun paints for me
and white shoes
the toes white as death
dead-white
east-west pointing toes

The bed behind is brass
the posts stern and phallic
the green satin cover
is frilled with white light

I can't breathe
the light, silvery, glittery
dapples the floor
flickering like fire
on the toffee boards

In the TV reflection
I am just legs and
a strip of black

Ophelia

Heavy rain
as heavy as my hope
dripping in buckets
like a clock

running down
the broken gutters
like flooding urine
from a drunk

Yesterday
I swam under a sky
as blue as agapanthus –
The sun fanned

in palm leaves
a bouquet'd Poinciana
drifted leaves like
confetti

jasmine bloomed
and hibiscus flared
unfurled skirts and
blood-dark throats

But there was only me
lifting my breast
extending my heart
in slow arabesque

poising for a Rubenstein
now dead.

Sadness came

Sadness came; depression settled
Like a weight anchoring my body
To the bottom of a draining bath

A crow flew across the sky
A black cut-out
In a slip of indigo cloth

The sun came up
A gilded coin
Balanced on a black card

The trees were quiet
Their stark skeletons
Charred with licking light

Addict

I shake my head
I can't risk
That again
Can I?
That darkness and despair
That bleak melancholy
That addiction to the gloaming

Because she *was* an addict
She wrote it herself
Addicted to writing
Addicted to words
Addiction is dangerous
Addiction is never good

Is it?

Addiction

The fountain pen
is filled like a syringe
you need to expel air
to get the ink to flow
to heal your
itchy heart
your longing for words
your restless
hatred of yourself
when you can't
write

What about me?

And me?
What about me?
Life is so much straighter
With Ginia sane

We work
We eat
We see movies
Visit friends

Go to the gym
Watch TV
Read
Sleep

I don't have a boyfriend
I don't have sex
I don't want a boyfriend
I don't want sex

Or I didn't…

Rub

Ah – but here's the rub
What right have I
To insist she stay this way
To not let her have her gift
To not let her have her drive
When it was the only thing
That made her feel
Whole?

When here is her chance –
Maybe a last –
To make her life
Fulfilled?

Simon…

Simon…

He wants Ginia
He could save her poetry
From disappearing altogether

But she would fall in love with him
I know
Without a doubt
He's attractive
He's intense

He wants her
Poetry
He wants her
For his film
He wants her

To go away
When it's over
Probably

Could she cope with that?
It could tip her

Into the death poetry
Again
Into death itself
Perhaps
Herself

Like Plath

Plath

No – not like Plath
Like Woolf
Plath was a coward
Woolf not so
She had so much more terror
Than Sylvia

Sylvia was a coward
Who can forgive her
Abandoning her children?
Practically leaving them to die
Because she wanted to punish Ted
Because she wanted to punish her father
Who was
Dead
Already
Anyhow

Woolf coped with so much more
When she was young –
Her mother's death
Her father's death
Her half-sister's death
Her brother's death
Abuse from her half-brothers

Then again

I guess Plath had no sister
To save her
Like Woolf had a sister –

Lovely Nessa
With her fine fingers
Mixing colours
Her paint-smeared cheek
Brown bare feet
Pattering restless rhythms
On cold tiles
Ear-lobes hanging pearls
Sea-washed and clean
Tangled in the twisted hair
On her long neck –

Like Ginia does

Dilemma

I finish my wine
Eat with the TV on

Think about Simon
About the film

Is it possible to make it
Without Ginia?

I squirm
I shake my head

I sigh
And the phone rings

Have you talked to her yet?
Has she made up her mind?

Geez – give me a break!
I haven't even washed the dishes yet!

Yeah, yeah – sorry it's just –
A job's come up

I'll be gone two, three weeks
Then I'd like to get stuck into it

With her
I can sort the sequence on the plane

Organise the guys
Organise some finance

I want to get this moving
You know?

I do know
I've seen him in action

He's focused
He's not fooling around

I'll visit her again, I say
Let you know, then

What if …

I go back to my veranda
Where the moon is sliding
Like a broken silver coin
Out of the murky muddy river-night

What am I to do?
I'm happy, aren't I?
Ginia's happy…
Isn't she?

If she comes back
Will she be different?
Will her gift even return
Anyway?

And what if
The film is a disaster?
Worse –
It doesn't even finish?

Can I risk it?
Can she?

Mind made

I shake my head
I grimace at the night
Because I know my mind
Is made up
Because hers is made
As it is
Come what may…

I shudder, silent sigh
Accept a little death

I know Ginia will fall for Simon
She will absolutely fall for Simon
As I've been falling for Simon

And all of that cannot be good

Part II

Waiting

It's been four weeks
Since Simon rang

Work is hectic
Summer's looming
I've begun to check my phone
Ginia's email
Often

But there's no message

Ginia's quiet
She hasn't asked after him
Since I told her he was gone

But I know she's been cutting back
On the pills
Taking half a dose

She thinks I don't know
But I see half-empty capsules
Pushed back into their foil

And I catch her reading
Her old poems
See her gaze into vacant space

See hope leap in her eye
When my mobile rings

And then his name is on it

Back

Hey! he says
I'm back! So much to tell!
Voice so excited
Ginia can hear

How's it going?
Is Ginia on board?
Because I gotta tell ya
I've got a crew on here!

Ginia's eyes widen
I feel my mouth go slack

Jen? Jenny? You there?

Yes. Yes I am.

Well?

I stare at Ginia
She stares back
Ginia is on board
I say slowly

Yes! Yes, I *knew* she'd be!
And she'll do a new book?
This is great! Really great!
Wait till you see what I've got.
Wait till Ginia sees it!
I'll fax a contract through!

I put the phone down slowly.
I'm still staring at my sister

And her eyes glaze
With tears
Tears.

Second meeting

We meet in the same café
A white drake has joined the ducks
I give Simon the contract
Ginia's signed

Allowing him to use her poems
Allowing him to use her voice
She will read aloud
In a studio

And she will have another
Book of poems
By the time
The film is aired

But then the clanger
She will not meet with him
She will not reveal her past
She is entitled

To her privacy

Thinking

I see him thinking
He wipes sweat from his flopping fringe
Rubs his eyelids with finger and thumb
Looks up at me

Frowns
Opens his mouth to speak
But I get in first

I will do the rest
I will be the filter
To protect her
And you will have your facts

But mystery too
Mystery is good, surely
In such a film?

Control

He's frowning
I see red threads of stress in his gaze
Defeat clouding the sky of his eyes

There is stubble on his jaw
A sheen of sweat on his bones
His lips are pressed closed

He wants control
Of course
It's his idea

But Ginia's my sister
And the poems are hers

Mystery is good
I repeat

He looks down again
Closes his eyes
Shakes his head

I need to think about it
It – it could work
I just – don't know

He cups his jaw
In long fingers with
Blunt nails

I look at his hands
Notice again
How strong and long they seem

Put out my own hand
Simon, I say
It's the only way

Ginia is not strong enough
For this yet
But I am

He meets my eye
Makes my heart jump

Okay, he says
We'll give it a go

Answers

So Simon has his answer
I've given him his answer

And Ginia has her answer:
She's coming off the drugs

I tell her that I know
I've seen the capsule foils

She tells me that she's fine
A bit of nausea, that's been all

But she wants to stop entirely
Today! She says, Today!

I say I'm not so sure
There's a warning on the packet

Large letters on the box –
DO NOT STOP TAKING THIS ABRUPTLY

She shrugs and says she'll risk it
How awful can it be?

I think she has a point
But Google to be certain –

And stare at her in horror.

No one told her

Going cold turkey

After fifteen months

Was going to be
Like coming off

Heroin

Side effects

We huddle on my bed
Read through my notes

Discuss the side effects
Of her return

The side effects
Of the potential film

All of it
Is terrifying

All of it
Is heart-stopping

All of it
She tells me

She can cope with

Now

Cold turkey

Ginia's sick
She throws up
Sweats the sheets wet
Her brain has electric shocks
Zaps
Which last seconds

She's hot
She's cold
She's moody
She's depressed

She takes downers
To take away the hours
To take away her mind
To get her through

Rages at me
While I sponge her face
Turns her back on me
When I offer food

Falls asleep
Strung out
On my lounge
In my bed

Happy

And then it's over.
She's clean
She's happy
She's suddenly sexy

She goes out with old friends
Picks up guys
Makes them laugh
Charms them

Her hair is soft
Her eyes are clear
She's slender
From the cleanse

She's back to one old self
The one of pre-teaching
The one of pre-Tess-death
Pain

I'm happy with her
We laugh at sit-coms
Analyse her conquests
Read her gentle starts

At new poems
A paddling
A dipping of the
Mind

Into music
And sensuality
And beauty
Again

And I begin to think,
Maybe Simon isn't everything
Maybe if the film
Falls through

She will
Still
Cope

Third call

He calls me four weeks later

He's staying in a unit
At the coast
While they film
He's not coming
Back to Brisbane
Till they've got
The sea poems done

Can we meet at Burleigh Beach?
He needs to write some background
Find the houses where she lived
Schools she went to, ballet halls
Places mentioned in the poems

I can see his need for this
But I hesitate, uncertain
How much will be revealed
By the people in those places?

Ginia's always been so private…

But I know it has to happen
Will have to take the risk
To trust in his integrity
And demonstrated skill

To shape my sister's life

Freedom

Waiting for him
At the Gold Coast
In the same café as last time
I watch the beach parade

How these Gold Coast people
Accept the freedom
Of voyeurism
The freedom from clothing

The freedom of the lifting
From gravity
Both literal and metaphoric
That the plunge into the ocean

Offers

To live by the sea
Is to accept freedoms
Rarely given elsewhere

Flirt

Jen!
I start from my reverie
Turn to see Simon
With his camera
Trained on me

Roll my eyes
And stand
Brush sand from my shorts
And my hands
Signal him to stop

But he doesn't
He's lively
Bubbly with energy
Flirty, I realize suddenly
He's flirting with me

With his camera
Making me laugh
And shake my head
Like he makes a model laugh…

Probably

I look straight into the lens
Tilt my head back
Strike a pose
Flick my hair

And he's delighted

Let's go to lunch, he says

Lunch

Is there anything more luscious
Than the sound of 'lunch'?
With its crackly, crunchy bite
Its promise of a picnic
Chocolate and crisp biscuit

He smiles when I order
Seafood basket
Salad on the side
He does the same
And orders wine

He's not here
For food only
But he's going to enjoy it
Nonetheless
He winks

Shift

To start with I am nervous
It's the intimacy
Or maybe

His azure eyes
Straight teeth
Dimpled grin

His taut butt
Flat belly
Long strong hands

He asks questions
And takes notes

As I answer
I twist my hands
Catch his eye
Look away too quickly

Notice that his writing slows
And he holds my gaze
Until I break it

Catch him
Not fully listening
Watching me

Then maybe it's the wine
Or maybe it's something else
But there's a shift between us

By the end of lunch
It's not business
Any more

He's flirting with me
And I'm flirting back
It's reflected in his eyes

Then I see him studying my face
In the film footage
Do you know

He says
You have a model profile?
The camera loves you

I shake my head
Watch him watch me

Blushing

Falling for him

Then my nerves are back
I glance at my watch
Exclaim I have to go

He pays the bill
Walks me to my car
Stands watching

As I bundle in my bag
Extends his hand
To thank me for my help

A warm hand
Warm smile
Warm *Call you soon*

Then I'm driving
On automatic
And the world has changed

Quiver

I can't help it
I thought I was free of this

I'd forgotten
This zing
This terror
This

Tsunami

I don't know how it's happened
One moment I was just flirting
In control, flattered

The next I'm
Lust-sick
Man-mad

Carrying my phone
Obsessively
Quivering to see

His name
On the screen
His voice in my ear

I thought I was free of this
I thought I was over it
I thought…

Don’t think

Don’t think
I scold myself
As the days go by
And there’s no call from him:

Watch a TV show
Go to the gym
Read a good book
But don’t think about him

Don’t think
That you *long* to meet him
That he *longs* to meet you
That Ginia *should* meet him –

Because Ginia’s calm
She’s really fine
Getting a life back
Not needing me so much

Not mentioning Simon
Or the film

I haven’t told her
About my lunch with him

Dream

We sat on a beach
Watching the water
Our hands were beside each other
I felt his little finger
Brush against mine
I looked up at his face

He took my hand
Put my finger in his mouth
Moved his tall frame to me
Took my mouth in his
Pressed his warm weight
Over me

Hands
Mouths
That's how it starts

I opened my eyes to darkness
Opened my breath to gasp
Opened my mind wide

Hands

His hands

Have slipped into my days
Between the sheets of
Humming faxes

Between the sheets
Of my bed
In my dreams

Between the leaves
Of my miniature lime
As I prune it

His hands

His long and graceful
Competent
And busy hands

Read

I come home with weekend shopping
Ginia's in the garden
Humming
I watch her through a window

The day is shatter-bright
Light hangs in gum leaves
Dapples pale mauve bark
Makes the lime leaves glow

A pony-tail palm thrusts fronds
In fountain ribbons
Catches blue beads she's strung
From a crooked branch

Pink and green strawberries bulge
Beside yellow-hearted flowers
And tomato leaves are
Feathers furred with spicy scent

There's cold coffee in the kitchen
Cake crumbs on the bench
A notebook on the table
Open

I pick it up
Read

In my head the words weave:
Whispering and withdrawing
They ebb and flow like a tide of sound.

There is a pain
At the base of my spine
Spinning like a thin current down my thighs

The crows caw
and a thin persistent chirp protests
The minahs squabble and…

The cherrrr of an engine slowing
Stutter, whirr, silence

Door creaking, slamming
The jingle of keys

A soft rap on timber

It's him

Him

I realise they're notes
Beginnings of poems
But –

Him? Him?
Who the hell is him?
Has something happened?

When did she write this?
I scrabble for a date
But there isn't one

I take the book
Agitated
Storm out to Ginia

What are you doing?
I yell
What have you been doing?

I thrust the book at her
She looks up from her weeding
Bewildered

She stands
Smears soil from her glove
On the page as she reads

Blushes scarlet
Oh, Jen,
This isn't real

I was imagining –
Someone – maybe this Simon –
Who likes my poems so much –

It's not real?
He didn't come here today?
You're not lying to me?

Oh Jen, Jen
What – no! Jen –
Why are you so upset?

Headspace

I stand, back to my bedroom door
Eyes closed
Trying to take it in
Trying to judge my feelings

I can't get Ginia out of my head
I can't get Simon out of my head
The more I think about him
The more space he gets

He's begun to invade my dreams
He's begun to kiss me in my dreams
He's begun to kiss Ginia in my dreams
Her dreams too, it seems

Looks

Ginia
It's her he wants to meet
It's always been her
That's why she haunts my mind

Instead it's me he's met
And he's made a move on *me*
It's clear he likes
My looks –

Which he knows are just like Ginia's…

But there's no harm
In me testing the water
Is there?

First move

I send him a text
Ask him out to lunch

To return the favour
And see how things are going

He will answer
I have no doubt

Have I?

Nothing

Don't

Panic

He may be
Asleep
At the movies
Out
With a girlfriend
In bed
With a girlfriend

Don't

It could all dissolve
Like the ending of a film

Don't!

Panic

Still nothing
What have I done?
Started something?
Or set myself up for pain
Again?

Or both?
I bite my nails
I sweat
I swallow gin

What have I done?

I imagine his hand on my hair
Lifting my face to his
My knees are weak

Will this really happen?

Why doesn't he
Answer me?

Buzz

And then the message comes

Great! Next Saturday at one
Okay with you?

I can't believe it
I can't believe this might be happening
I'm buzzing
Charged with desire
And daring
Dying to meet him again
Dying to touch him
Taste him

I'm alive
Happy
Looking forward to the day
Looking forward to meeting him
In a bar
In a restaurant
Anywhere
I can seduce
Him

Scarlet

We meet in a bar
I wear scarlet
I see his eyes startle
Oh yeah, interest there

It's easy really
A red dress
Red lipstick
Make the difference

Mean you're hot
Mean you're up for it
Mean forget Ginia
Look at me

He has her book
Open in his hand

He closes it

Palms

Let me read your palm, I say
He holds his right one out
I shake my head
You're right-handed
I need to read the left
first

Why's that?

Your left shows the potential
You were born with
The right what you've made
Of your life
So far

Oh

He is obedient
Proffers his left palm
I take it
Warm
In my two hands
My heart tremors
I am touching him

I am touching him

I take my time
Wanting this contact
To never finish

I take a breath
Force myself to concentrate
I measure his fingers
Against his palm
Look at his finger lengths
His colour

Pink, I say
That's good
And your palm long
As your fingers
You're a water

Water? Puzzled

There are four signs –
Earth, air, water and fire

He smiles
Amused
Humouring me

And that means?

I meet his eye
Still holding his hand in both mine
I hope he can't feel
The pulse of my heart

You're creative
Perceptive
Sympathetic
You do things intuitively

I don't add
Sometimes moody and introverted
Sometimes emotionally inhibited
Sometimes withdrawn
That's for me to know
To store
For future use

I look down at his hand again
Next is the heart line
There are four:
Heart, head, life and fate
I say

My own heart quickens
The line is long and curvy

Emotionally expressive
I murmur

Now the head line
Which is deep and long

Your thinking is clear and focused

The lifeline
Curvy

Plenty of energy

Lastly the fate
Broken and erratic

Prone to many changes from life

I hold his hand
Then look up at him slowly
He is watching my face

I lift his hand
To him
Let my hands fall

Would you like me to read
The other one
At my place?

Seduction

I lead him into the house
I'm babbling
I've said I'll show him other poems
Drafts Ginia hasn't finished

Do you want some coffee?
Will I get the poems first?
Or maybe a beer?
Please – take a seat – out on…

I stop mid-sentence
He's leaning on the kitchen bench
I can see the bulge
In his pants

Jenny
Softly
Jen
What are you doing?

I turn, stare at him
Am I doing something?
I feel a smile
Flutter on my mouth

He puts out a hand
And touches my arm
Goosebumps
My smile is gone

My lips are parted
My heart is hammering
My fingertips are hot
My throat is raspy

His hands are on my waist
His breath is on my face
His beery breath and warm, wet mouth
Eat me

His hands move over my skin
Under my blouse
Up to my breasts
In their new bra

He moans a sigh
Do you have to be so tantalizing?
When you're not Ginia…

(*Forget Ginia!*)

You have crept into my dreams
These breasts have crept into my dreams

Then we have met in our dreams
Both, in our dreams
I am whispering

His eyes are closed
My hands are on his buttocks
His groin is pressed to mine

I have watched you too
This bum
Do you know that?

My blouse is off
He's fumbling with my bra clip
I have him unzipped

Ginia is eclipsed

Pillow talk

Later, he tells me about his life
How he was born in Scotland
Came with his parents here
When he was eight

The landscape shocked him
After frozen winters
Spiked with stalactites of ice
Snow spread in vast sheets
Settling like padded cotton
Throws

Gumboots for outdoors
Plimsolls for in
Multistorey classrooms
With tarred school yards

To sun-popping tin roofs
Gusts of hot-breathed wind
Brown-grassed paddocks
And shimmer-rippled
Ankle-deep
Heat

How could he love
A sun-burned country?

It was only when they moved to the sea
To green-glass waves
And salt-scented sunshine
A coastal school
On the edge of the ocean
A camera

That he began to see

And it is the sea-poems
He loves the most
He says –
What drew him to my sister
What inspired his vision
Of the film

Don't ask

He lifts himself on an elbow
Rests his head on one hand
Strokes my cheek with the other

I think he wants to ask
About meeting her again
But checks himself –

Sees maybe it's unwise
Right now
Instead he says

He has to go
Has to be at the sound studio
At four o'clock

I nod, Of course,
I smile and touch his fingers
To my lips

Watch him dress
Hear the door click
After him

Next

So, what will come next?
I shower and dress
Pour myself a drink
Think of Ginia

My heart turns over
Oh, my lord

What have I done?
Of course
She's been shyly waiting
For me to introduce him –

For who would not be eager
To meet a flattering fan
And such a good-looking one
As I've described to her?

You don't have to be male
For sex to waltz in
When the door of admiration
Opens

But perhaps you must be female
To dream that love
Might be its partner
Every time

Tidy

I tidy up the bed
Put on a load of washing
Iron clothes for work
Finish up my weekend chores

Sweep Simon
Into a jewelled compartment
In my head
Decide I won't tell Ginia

Anything

Part III

Hail

Dawn, and hail lightly clicking
On the iron roof
The light sea-green
By eight a.m. it's a torrent

The kitchen grey as a kitten
The hail bouncing like popcorn
Convex discs
Clattering like ice bullets

Then sunlight and the grass
Covered with silver coins
Steam flowing knee-deep
On the black river of bitumen

Weekday morning
And I've hardly slept
Simon hasn't called
He hasn't answered my texts

It's been more than two weeks

Jerk

It's Saturday eight a.m.
Ginia is at peace
Finding inspiration

Is in her room
Flicking through
Old poems
Old photos
Old memories

I'm drinking tea in bed
Reading the papers
And someone raps on the door

I start
Could it be…it couldn't possibly be…
Simon?

Surely not
He wouldn't just turn up
Without calling first

Would he?

I pull on a silk robe
Look at my naked face
Oh hell

Louder raps

Oh, well

If I'm going to scare him off
It might as well be
Now –

Jack

I stare at him
Feel my heart jerk
Feel my face flush

Hey, Jen
Mind if I come
In?

Shock

I am breath-taken
I can't think
My mind slow as sludge

From the shock of his hazel eyes
Toothpaste smell
Aries tattoo

From expecting someone else
What was I thinking?
Answering the door in my robe

Answering the door at all
At eight o'clock on a Saturday
When all normal people are sleeping in

When all normal people wouldn't dream
Of shocking you half to death
With the past

Back

He wants me back
He's heard Ginia's sane
And he wants me back

He sits across the table from me
His eyes bright and keen
His new-washed hair still wet

He's lonely
He misses me
He wants to try again

He wants to take me to breakfast
To talk to me
To talk me into it

He loves me
He still loves me
And I still love him, don't I?

I have to give him a second chance
Give us a second chance
We were so good together

He's thinking of buying a house
He wants me to see it with him
He wants me to move back in with him

He goes through the real estate paper
As I shower and dress
Make up

He chats through the closed door
As if we've never been apart
As if we're a couple

Again

Breakfast

Jack is charming
Jack has always been charming
He takes me out to eat

He pulls out my chair
Orders coffee the way I like it
Orders eggs the way I like them

Everything is so familiar
His hands drawing shapes in the air
The crease in his cheek when he smiles

His voice quick as water
The gold flecks in his eyes
The starched panels of his crisp shirt

He works in insurance
Has the salesman's knack
Of disarming you

Taking your cartridges
While you don't even notice
The gun is gone

Wolf

Past love
Walks beside you
Like a wolf,
Hounds you
Nips at your memories
Howls in your dreams

I watch his face
Feel his fingers on my hand
Start at the remembered touch
Of love lost
Lost life
Together

Offering

There's a house he's excited about
A run-down Queenslander
He can see transformed
Fresh paint
Polished floors
Opened decks

Glimpses of the city
A poinciana-shaded yard
Room for a pool
He knows I'm a sucker
For Queenslanders
For trees

He's offering it all
Stability
Security
Serenity
A future
Together

So long, of course,
As Ginia doesn't come
Too

Think about it

He drops me home
I don't ask him up
I'm silent
Which uneases him

He covers it with bluff
Tells me he has to go
Appointments
Even on a Saturday

Tells me breezily
To think about it

His last glance
Gives him away

A flash of fear
In the gold-flecked green
Catches my heart
I know him so well

I do
I always will

Love him
My first real love

But I have to protect
Ginia

Don't I?

And now
Of course
There's Simon
Too…

Break

I need to have a break
I need to get away to clear my head
Sort out what I want
What is good for me
Good for Ginia

I pack a bag
Tell Ginia I'm off to Straddie
To visit Mum and Dad
Ask if she wants to come

She nods
After a moment
There's that old guilt
That old fear
Of dragging pain in our parents' eyes

But I'll be with her
I'll protect her
I grab my camera
Hand it to her

Take a pic a day
I tell her
To write a poem about
Get you started, get you going
Keep that old brain working

She smiles at me
Yes, she says
Good idea
You have such good ideas

Trip back

We catch a water taxi to the island
A new bus meets us there
Summer-sky blue
Air-conditioned, roomy

We stash our bags
And sit behind the driver
Memories tumble past:
Tangled vines in eucalypts

Sandy black-flecked soil
The Dunwich Cemetery
Where my grandparents
And sister Tess

Have plaques
Nan and Pop are buried there
But we sprinkled Tess's ashes
On the sea

She loved the sea
A dozen dolphins swam
Where the ashes fell
Carrying her soul

We like to think
To their secret caves
And clean, crisp currents
Where she might be reborn

We pass the turn to Amity
Where Nan and Pop
Lived out their lives
Rumble on to Cylinder

Island lunch

I'd forgotten
What old hippies they regressed to
When they were at the beach
Mum in her bathers and a wrap
Dad in fish-spattered shirt
And balding straw hat

No more suits and ties
Management meetings
For him
Or classrooms full of
Teenage angst
For her

There's a hammock slung
Between two palms
Books littered with acacia flowers
Dad's built a henhouse
And the birds bob and peck
Weave like plump, uncertain dancers

Dad had the boat out at dawn
Has caught red snapper
Crabs and calamari
He fires up the barbie
Mum makes salad
Scoops avocado and early mango

I open wine I've brought
Ginia sets the table
Spreads a cloth
Napkins and side plates
For crusty bread
From the island bakehouse

We eat, compliment the cooks
Avoid mentioning
Tess
I don't tell them about Simon
The doco
Or Jack wanting back

New life

They seem so steady now
Our parents
Where once she was so prickly
Hurt by his neglect
And he her razor tongue
Which shamed him

Now he raves about the dawn
The boat sliding in a milky silver sea
Mangroves ghostly in the breaking light
Dolphins gliding at the bow
A sunrise painted
In gaudy pink and gold

He pours another beer
Tops up our wine
Mum fetches fruit
Tells us about the neighbours
An artist and a gardener
Brings out her beads

She threads crystals as she talks
Droplets of cerulean-blue
Amber glass with strands of gold
Her nimble fingers flash
The gemstones into jewels
To sell at Sunday's market

Strings of bells
On roped red and yellow yarn
Sickle-shaped moons
In heavy gold brass
She's been making cakes as well
Has pots of chutney, jars of jam

From next door music drifts
On blue incense
Leonard Cohen's
'Hallelujah'
Mournful and yearning
Lullaby song

Makes us all yawn
Makes Dad take to the hammock
Mum go for a lie-down
Ginia and I do the dishes
Then take towels and the camera
To the beach

Home beach

Home Beach is my favourite
With its oily violet pools
Its fringe of white tree trunks
Washed clean by waves

We know better than to forage
For driftwood and shells
In those stark stands
With their ghostly rustles

Sharp peppery scent
And moving shadows –
Have stabbed our feet before
On buried branches

Broken shells
Tough twigs resistant
To the briny high-tide douse
Of feather-fingered sea

We dump our towels and shirts
Take courageous breaths
Dive beneath the green skin
Of a rearing, roaring roller

Lines

I dry off on my towel
Perch on my elbows
Belly-down and salty-skinned
Watch Ginia snap pics

I remember her remark:
Nothing in nature is a straight line
Even the she-oak leaves
Have a slight curve

And are mussed together anyway
So the lines are blurred
Only light is straight
Clean as scissor blades

Cutting out charming
Shadow patterns
Which of course
Have no straight lines at all

This is perhaps why, I think
Buildings blocked in brick
Without a curve
Seem so ugly

Why we love an arch
A curly filigree of iron lace
Bumpy opaque glass
A sweep of suspended curtain

Why I love my parents' beach-house
With its sandy grass
Shaded by messy gums
And lush underbrush

I drift to sleep
In the warm sun
With the hush of waves
To lull me

Voices

I wake to find
Ginia flopped beside me
She clicks out her new stones
And her new pics

Then tells me her news

She's heard music
Echoing once more
In her head
From a radio long lost

Drinking wine at lunch
Listening to our parents' voices
Listening to mine
She heard her own again

At last

And she has a new poem

Muse

She comes with a sliver
of light
a silver bead
of water
sliding in a leaf's furrow
the slightest silence
after the murmur of sleepy sparrows

She comes with the crushed
felt of a petal
dropped on wet soil
the heavy hit
of cut grass and damp earth
the breath of tomato leaves
rubbed like fragrance on the fingers

She comes with a hot loaf
and sweet crabmeat
crunchy calamari
the bite of chardonnay
snap of snow peas
the lick of olives
on oiled lips

She comes with a piano
and afternoon drowsiness
the plink of memories
tongue-thick
the rush of wind
creak of iron

the piano like a voice

I know

This is it
I *know*
It's time for Ginia
To meet Simon

She wants to
Badly
I see it in her face
Her wordless gaze

And this is Ginia
At her best
This is Ginia
Misty and warm

Dreamy and beautiful
Able to charm
The coils from a
Viper

Let alone
A thirty-year-old
Obsessed with her poetry
And its author

But…

But –
I am luck-sucked
He hasn't called
Hasn't sent a text

I don't trust him
How can I trust him?
If he does this to me
How would Ginia cope?

Oh, the risk could be too great
Sure it's Ginia he wants
Not me
But even so

If he should hurt her
Upset the fragile balance of her mind
It could all end
In more than tears

I'm the sane one
I'm rational and clear-headed
I'm the one to make the right decision

And then Jack's back

He's offering everything
And if I say okay
But only if Ginia has a place
In our lives too…

Oh, vague, vain hope!

I stare at her
Feel tears sting my eyes
Take her hand
Tell her I love her poem

Night

The night is hard and white
Moon too bright
Flaring on wind-whipped waves
And ghost-gum trunks

I've wandered out alone
To see the black and white
Dispel the seething grey
Of doubt and fear

I should do this, I think,
As I draw my mobile out
Simon so wants –
But has not met –

The real Ginia after all…
I have to take a chance
Give her that chance
Give *them* that chance

I bring up his number

Sheepish

Hey Jen
Sheepish

Simon
I'm ice-cream cool
Guess what?
I'm ringing about Ginia

Look, Jen, I –

Guess what?
She's meeting you
Give me a time
Place
She'll be there

Jen, Jen –

Just text it to me
Okay?

I click off
Shaking
Clench my eyes
Feel my heart
In my fingertips

Professional

I wave Ginia off
She smiles back nervously
But I've grilled her on what
And what not to say

I've been professional
Advised on the parameters
Of her involvement
In the film

The rest of course
I leave to her
She knows nothing
Of that afternoon

I told him that
And that I was going back to Jack

There was only silence
Except for breathing

Jack again

Well, what's to stop me
Going back
To Jack?

With any luck Ginia's
Off my hands
For good

And I am free to live my life
With a good man
Who loves me

Loves *Jen*
Not Ginia

Not *both of us…*

Holiday weekend

Jack invites me to Caloundra
To the Honeymoon House
Well that's what we called it
On our first trip away
In fact a beach shack
With powder-pale walls
Creaking floorboards
Smell of insecticide and Ajax

Where we tangled
Through the *Kama Sutra*
On long hot afternoons
While fine sand creased in
Sheets and rusting fans whipped
Wind across our sunburn
Then we ate in beach cafés
And walked on moonlit sand

But the shack's no longer there
Swept away for high-rise flats
With ocean views
Cool tile floors
Sunken spa baths
A pool and gym
Because the world has turned
Too far away from then

And we should both have known
The past can never be
The future

Bad start

Then we can't find a room
We've picked a bad weekend
Streets clogged with bikes
And joggers
In some race

Jack barks at traffic
Swears at blocked roads
Finds a free room at last
In a back street hotel
With brick wall views

Unpacked, we try the pool
I'm cautious
But Jack scoffs
And yanks me in

A bad start

A tall pubescent boy
With bad bleached hair
Taunts his bleating brother
Flips him under water
Latched arms like locks

A spa frets and hisses

The children's mother
Sprawls
Belly bulging
In a wide two-piece

Her cocked knees rock
As she reads
And when she rolls
Red stripes paint her back
From the white plastic lounge

A big-bummed girl
With caffè latte skin
Saunters past
In coconut-ice

She plunges

The little brother
Is released
Swims, coughing
To the edge
His appeal

Forgotten

I think of Ginia
And what she's said
Of Simon

Surprise

She likes him
Likes what he's done
With film

He likes her voice
Uses her silhouette
But not her face

Just like he promised me
And then I asked
Does she – you know –

Find him…a flirt?
And she frowned and said:
Oh yes. But he would want too much…

Then she took my hand
Her fingers warm and soft
Told me to go back to Jack

If that was what I wanted
Her new book
The film

Were enough for her
Now
She could cope

Without me

End

So I guess that's it
What more have I to say?

The film was picked up
By a network
It's good
It's had rave reviews

Ginia's second book
Is sold out
And she's started on another
This time about the mountains

Which is a relief
Too much talk of water
And her stones
Has always frightened me

As for me
I'm much the same
Learned there was no
Going back to Jack

And no leaving Ginia
Find we complement each other
I work less
Now she has money coming in

And her writing
Makes me tranquil

Feel at times I'm fading
Now that Ginia's so strong
And doesn't need me any more
But that's only momentary

Because I know her
Through and through
Know even when she's strong
She's still as fragile as a bird

Underneath
And when she crumples
I'll be back as tough as ever
To save her

Again.

www.ingramcontent.com/pod-product-compliance
Lightning Source LLC
Chambersburg PA
CBHW071845080526
44589CB00012B/1114

9781740278737